girl
(remastered)

jessica jocelyn

girl (remastered)

illustrations by: Janelle Parraz
edited by: Tarah Threadgill

to all the people who keep their stickers in a safe place
until they find the perfect spot for them.

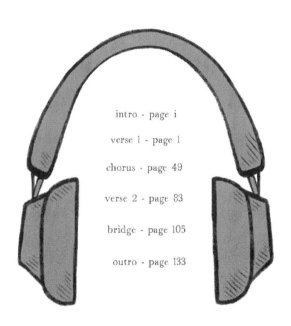

a lot was harmed
during the making of the girl
you see before you.
I gravitate towards the sun
while mascara
runs down my cheeks.

verse 1

jessica jocelyn

girl (remastered)

in our love story,
two things were true:
we were breathlessly in need
of each other's souls
and
we filled each other's pockets
with rocks
while we were drowning.

it was just a normal day
and casually speaking,
you told me you had a book
you wanted to give me,
but that it didn't come out
for 12 more days.

you can't say things like that.
not to a girl
who hyper-fixates on kind words.
not to a girl
who doesn't know a thing
about her father's new family.

to you it was just:
  here, I saw this and thought of you.
to me, it sounded like:
  when I write the pages of my future
  I'll make sure there is a place for you.

girl (remastered)

I don't know how
to love quietly,
meekly,
sweetly.
I only know
how to run full-speed
straight into burning buildings,
bursting down the walls.
I don't know how
to tell you this softly,
but I will shout about our love
until my lungs burn
for their next breath.

talking long into the night,
watching the stars
come out one by one.
eyes burning from
the need to sleep,
I know I'll find it hard
to wake up tomorrow.
but I'll give up these hours of sleep
just to spend it
talking and laughing with you.

I don't believe our love
could move mountains,
but I'm sure it could transcend
this world to the next
and the next after that.
there was never a time
when my heart didn't know yours.
it will find you
after every death
and breathe into you
each new life
just to experience *us*
all over again.

we never had to speak.
it was the best
and worst thing about us.
maybe you could sense
I wasn't any good at it.
all my life,
I felt maybe I wasn't from this planet,
and when your bare skin
was on mine,
it was the most human
and connected to the earth
I ever felt.

sometimes I can't stand you.
other times,
I don't think I deserve you.
both times,
I don't want
to be without you.

girl (remastered)

run with me
so fast,
we forget all this,
forget everything
we're told,
everything
they say.

you are
a mausoleum of broken dreams
and one too many
"i'm so sorry- i'll never do it again"
conversations at 2 a.m.

girl (remastered)

when will
we ever learn?
this road always leads
to the same place.
we've been here before
and we'll just end up
there again.

these secrets and memories
I tell you,
they aren't ammunition
ready for you
to fire back.
they are ways
to learn to love me,
not targets for you to hit
to make sure
I come crashing down.

girl (remastered)

I'm drowning under the weight
of loving you.
just as I swim back
to the surface,
you steal my breath
and pull me back under.

I wish I had known
that your demons
would fascinate me,

calming me with
skeleton fingers,
twirling strands of my hair,

that I wouldn't know
how to navigate life
without them,

that I wouldn't
recognize myself
when they left.

girl (remastered)

I screamed at the moon
and demanded to be shown
where it all went wrong.

she blew into the sky
and when the clouds cleared,
I saw you
grabbing my hand
for the first time.

my heart
is a wound
yet to be healed.
I think that's how
you keep
getting
back
in.

girl (remastered)

it breaks my heart,
but I know
if I want you to be happy,
I need to walk out the door
and not come back.

we're hiding from
our past ghosts
and pretending
we're good people.

like our kisses
didn't leave graveyard chills
and the wounds on our backs
didn't come from
each other's knives.

like my blood
isn't still under your nails
and mine is not still
under yours.

everyone makes mistakes;
it's all in being human.
it's not the mistakes
that I judge you for.
it's everything that came after
that broke me.

the two hardest sentences
in the english language
for you are:
I'm sorry.
I was wrong.

I think if I had gotten that,
everything would be different
right now.

I can't be the darkness
in you anymore.
I can't stand smelling
like your regret,
or have your tears
burning on my skin.

imagine,
just imagine
how we could be together
if we both healed.

I can't tell
if it's me
or if it's you
flying this plane
spiraling
out of control,
but I'm begging you
please save us.

with a finger to my lips,
you stop the words
from coming,

the ones you know
that will tell you to go.

the thing is, I know I can live without you. I know this. I just don't want to have to. how can you ask that of me when I know the warmth of your hands on my body? now that I know what it feels like to be loved by you? how can you ask me to live the rest of my life knowing what all that feels like while knowing I'm *never* allowed to experience it again?

when all was said and done,
there are parts of me,
parts of us,
that just didn't survive
when I followed you
through these broken roads.

I don't want
to get rid of the anger.

it's all
I have
left of you.

I want to go back

back to when I first learned
what your name was,
back to when we talked about
favorite colors and favorite movies,
back to when I learned
your pet peeve was bad parking
and you found out mine
was misspelled words,
back before I learned
you got angry
when you felt shame,
and back before
you learned
I destroy people
before they can ever destroy me.

girl (remastered)

I know we both get lost
in what should've happened between us,
what we should've done,
what we should've been.
every *what if*
feels like a razor blade
to my wrist.
it doesn't matter
what should've happened,
because at the end of the day
it didn't happen
and I can't keep feeding myself
hypothetical dreams
that will never come true.

when you left,
I knew I would miss you.
but what I ended up
missing most
was who I was
when you were near.
the way I laughed,
smiled,
danced.
I realized I wasn't chasing after you.
I was chasing the girl
I used to be.

girl (remastered)

I will wander till
the end of time,
missing a piece of my heart,
the piece I tucked
in your pocket
when we said goodbye.
please don't ever
try to find me.
I don't want it back,
I want it
with you.

I'm hoping one day
you come back,
but not in the way
you usually would.
maybe in the shadows
of my periphery,
or in those final moments
before I come back
to consciousness
from my dreams.

girl (remastered)

sometimes I write to remember
and
sometimes I write to forget.
somewhere in the middle
of all that,
there you stay.

when I hugged you goodbye,
I felt if
my tears mixed with yours,
perhaps somehow
they would fall to the ground
and grow a new world
where it was possible
we could still be together.

I love you.
I do.
with all of my being.
but
this lifetime
just doesn't
belong to us.

if you must go
then go.
but before you leave
let me have one more night.
I want to memorize
every mark,
every curve.
press your palms
so hard against my skin
that your fingerprints
brand me
and can never be erased.
let me love you one last time
and let's be honest,
maybe the only way
I ever really knew how.

girl (remastered)

we will end where we began:
simply strangers.

on an old dirt road
our song comes on.
and for those four minutes
and seven seconds,
I allow you in.
I feel you in the passenger seat
and become immersed
in your laughter.
I permit myself
to live in a timeframe
where you are still in love with me.
I let myself remember your touch,
our jokes,
our life together.
when the guitar stops,
I force you to leave
and your face is erased
from my mind.
but for those four minutes
and seven seconds,
I allow you love me again.

in another time and place
I don't carry the scars
from my childhood into the future
and you have none to bring with you either.
my mother loves me right
and yours accepts you
for who you are.
no lies slip off your tongue
and everything you speak,
you mean.
I love you with an innocence
and you love me back,
not taking advantage of it.
we don't bury each other with hate
because we've actually been taught
how to love.
in another time and place,
we make it.

or maybe in another time and place
we are both on a crowded street,
walking with the flow
of other people
and for a brief second
our eyes meet
and although we feel like
we need to stop
and introduce ourselves,
we keep walking
and go on to create beautiful lives
not chained and bound
by the trauma we caused each other.

I say
I did my best,
but what I mean is
I wish I had loved myself
like I do now.
loved myself enough
to walk away
the first time.
loved myself enough
to take the first
red flag seriously.
loved myself enough
to not sacrifice my soul
just because I thought
I didn't deserve more.

maybe it would be easier
if I knew how much
you hurt without me,

if I knew how badly
you wanted to touch my face
or call just to hear my voice.

maybe it would be easier
if I knew you
still dream about me
and wake up wishing
I was still next to you.

maybe it would be easier
if I knew inside
you were dying, too.

take me to an August
that never hurt,
an August that doesn't shake me awake
from nightmares.
take me to an August
filled with love and laughter.
take me to an August
that doesn't have anniversaries
of death and trauma.
take me to an August
where I still believed in magic.
take me to an August
where I was thankful
to just be breathing.

breathing hurts now.

suddenly there's September.
hopefully it brings things
that August couldn't.

though I can't help but wonder
as I watch the leaves descend,
if I could shed and fall to pieces as well
and show up brand-new
and beautiful
next spring.

I feel like trying again.

the love I have for you
eats at my flesh,
but the hate I feel
disintegrates my soul.
it's destroying me,
feeling either love or hate.
either way, I lose.
to be free,
I need to feel nothing for you.
to be able to pass you by on the sidewalk
and not think twice,
not even blink.
I need to be able to hear your name
and not even bat an eyelash.
to be free,
I need to not love or hate you.

I need to feel nothing.

jessica jocelyn

.

chorus

jessica jocelyn

I know each time
my father's hand
strikes my face,
he thinks
he's helping me learn
and be tougher
for the world.
how awful
to know
that he had to have been
just as small as I was
when he was taught
that this is how
you show love.

my father's love
became a knife
lodged in my back.
I could never decide
between
letting it stay
and living with the pain,
or removing it
and bleeding to death.

girl (remastered)

just between us
(and I won't tell your new daughter)
was it more emotional
when I was born?
did you cry because I was your first?
is every sight, smell, and sound
ingrained in your memory?

just between us
(and I won't tell your new wife)
do you think my mom is prettier?
did she give better hugs and tell better jokes?

just between us
(and I won't tell your new family)
do you think about my sister and I
before you go to sleep?
do you wonder if we ever went to college
or what our favorite movies are?

just between us
(and I won't tell anyone else)
is there a void in your heart
just like there is in mine?
do you cry yourself to sleep sometimes
wondering what your life
would've been like if you had stayed?

just between us
did leaving us destroy you, too?

it was never about attention
and it was never
about dying
when I made those marks
running side to side
on my arm.
I felt so dead inside
but needed to make sure
and
the pain
was how
I knew
I was still alive.

I am the oldest daughter,
a soldier whose number
came up for the draft,
chosen to experience
the brunt of the fist
so my siblings
might receive a lesser blow.

I am the oldest daughter,
a mountain
that pretends she is not crumbling,
made to learn the lessons first
so my mistakes
can be a guide for them.

I am the oldest daughter
and now they have to live without me.
tearing my heart equally,
I give each of them a piece
with a promise:
I'll come back for you.

my heart breaks
knowing that they can't come
and their hearts break
realizing I can't stay.

as a child,
your words became chains.
they held me to the ground
to make sure
I could never take flight.

I grew older and stronger.
link by link,
I unchained myself.
unchained us.
deconstructing from the religion of you,
of our family.

sometimes blood
isn't thicker than water
because it's been diluted
with poison.

a Christmas story you may have never heard:

bright and early, my younger sisters and I wake up and run to the tree. we are tired from not sleeping. the tree is brightly lit, and my step-father starts a fire; it was always something that he was good at. he could get it lit quickly and keep it going. we all sit around opening presents and he gets out the video camera to record our reactions. my new orange kitten, Milo, plays in the sea of crumpled paper. my step-father cracks jokes as we laugh and compare presents. he and my mother look at us lovingly and then look at each other the same way. for that day, and only one day a year, I close my eyes and can almost imagine that we are normal. that my parents are in love and they don't hate each other. that my mother has healed her wounds and knows how to protect us from her unhealed parts. that my step-father can express his anger instead of using his fists to prove a point. that we can go to our grandmother's house later and truly be the happy family that we portray. for this day and this day only, we can pretend we are okay.

the hardest pill I've ever
swallowed
was learning
that the people
who are supposed to love us
sometimes
just
don't
know
how.

my childhood best friend
had four legs and the kindest brown eyes.
he didn't mind if we never talked
and never laughed at me
when I cried.
he'd just sit there next to me
and let me hug him for as long as I needed to.
he chased me through sprinklers
and summer heat
and when I scratched myself on a pinecone
he had given me,
I think he was genuinely sorry.
many years passed,
he got older and his eyes became gray.
when his body became too tired,
he went behind my mother's chair
and laid down to rest for a final time.
I touched his cold, sweet head
and marveled how
such a simple creature
could teach me more
about deep love and deep loss
than any human had yet.

I sometimes wonder
if deep down,
I hated having my father's last name
so much
that
I wanted to change it
the first chance I could.

girl (remastered)

I used to think
that my father
was gone for good
when he walked away.

but he's everywhere.

he's in how I jump
when a door
slams a bit too loud.

he's the burn
of the lies
on my tongue
sliding out
just a bit too easily.

he's in the way
I never trust anyone
and just expect them to leave.

I used to think he was gone for good
when he left,
but he's still everywhere.

when my mother
was forming
in my grandmother's womb,
there I was being molded
as well.
an egg,
sitting next to a million others
inside my mother,
listening in
on the daily life
of a 1950s housewife
and soaking in her codependence.
being conditioned
to flinch at trauma
that wasn't even meant for me.
maybe this is why
I hold my children extra tight at birth,
trying to soothe all
that they
have already
experienced.

girl (remastered)

my parents
never stood up
to the unhealed
versions inside themselves
and ended up
passing the torch
of generational trauma
down to me.

I had no idea
I was carrying it
until I looked into
my baby's eyes
for the first time
and felt the weight
of me holding on to it.

they told me
once I had children,
especially one like me,
that I would understand them more.
but now I do.
and I understand them even less.

my daughter came out screaming
and didn't stop for a year straight.
I used to think that was a bad thing.
she got older
and started to dance and sing.
if she got caught by a stranger,
she'd pause for a second
but stare them straight in the eye
and continue.
she came into the world loud.
she came into the world purging
the anguish
of a woman trying desperately
to feed and clothe her children
during the Great Depression.
the anguish
of a woman who lost her son
in battle during WW2.
the anguish of a mother
who buried an empty casket
because her son never came home
from Vietnam.
the anguish of a woman
who slaved away
in front of a stove all day
only for her husband to come home
and tell her he didn't care
for the pie she made.
the anguish of a woman
who allowed a man to break her
again and again
just so she'd have food to eat.
the anguish of a woman
who came to this country
in hopes of a better life

for her children than she had.
my daughter came out screaming
and didn't stop for a year straight.
I used to think this was a bad thing.
but her voice released
all the women before her
and set their spirits free.

how lucky am I
that I get to love you?
I get to show you
how life is lived.
you'll go farther
than I ever could
and see things
that I'll never see.
but, still
how lucky am I
that I get to have you
until my time is done?

I know you by heart.
I've memorized every freckle,
every speck of gold
in your eyes.
in a room full of people,
I'd still be able
to pick out your cry.
and if my sight
was ever taken,
I'd know your face
with my hands.

girl (remastered)

sitting on the bathroom floor
I watch my husband paint
our daughter's nails.

how different my life
would've been
if I'd had that.

one day I saw
my child's face
and started to see my own,
started to hear my laughter,
started to see my own smile.
a precious soul
wrapped in mortal blood and bones
but reflecting all
I needed to fix
and all I needed
to embrace about myself.
to have a child
is to look at yourself in the mirror
and every day
improve what you see.

when I became a mother
I was prepared for everything
but the rage.

the rage of seeing how easy
it was to love someone
so small
so helpless,

the rage of knowing how easy
it was to step back
and swallow my anger
when they did something "wrong."

when I became a mother,
I was prepared for everything
but the rage.

my children sometimes ask
and want to know
where I came from.

they want to know
where I got my brown eyes
or who taught me
how to do my make-up.

it hurts to tell them
that my brown eyes came from a man
I know nothing about.

and that it was me
sitting alone in my room,
figuring it all out.

as a woman,
it's hard to win.
we grow up and have children
but aren't allowed to talk about
how we miss life before them
or how tired we are.
or if we grow up and decide not to have them,
then there must be something wrong with us
and we're just being selfish.
if we stay home to raise them,
then we are lazy and don't contribute much.
but if we have a career,
then what kind of woman are we
to leave our children to grow
with someone else?
as a woman,
it's just so hard to win.

maybe in another time,
in another universe,
there is a little girl
with long, dark hair
and she is loved right
by the people who were supposed
to love her.

she lies in fields of flowers
and butterflies dance on her cheeks
and the burn from the sun
is the most painful thing
she ever feels.

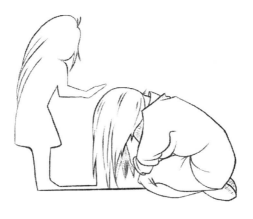

I think a lot of us
were born to people
who had children just because
they thought
it's what you're supposed to do.

they didn't realize we'd
come out so noisy and messy
and become walking mirrors
showing them everything
they hated inside themselves.

we became filed
deep within their "failures" folder
a part of their life they wish
they could do over,
but skip the part where we come in.

I think a lot of us
were born to people
who only wanted us
because they thought
they were *supposed* to.

the thing no one tells you about when you have children is the fact that you will relive your childhood and all that trauma you experienced will come back up to the surface, demanding to be acknowledged and felt. it will hit you one morning as you get up and make them breakfast and help them get dressed, you will take a step back and sometimes it takes your breath away. you will fight ghosts and demons and constantly look in the mirror, convinced you are failing. but then, in the middle of the night, one of them will come to you with a nightmare, and instead of yelling at them to go back to sleep, you will walk with them back to their bed, and explain to them that you have nightmares, too, and what helps you fall back asleep. you'll watch them play and laugh and your heart will ache for the childhood you never had but deserved. sometimes you'll cry and wonder why you were treated the way you were. the depression will set in sometimes.

yet...

you will realize that with every passing day, you are breaking generational curses. that you are using your own parental wounds to ensure that there aren't going to be more human beings walking this earth with their own.

if I could,
I'd go back to the day
my father was born
and love him.
really love him.
I would take him in my arms
and raise him as my own.
I would give him more
than a dog squeak toy for his birthday.
I'd give him gentle discipline
and hug him every day
but also teach him about consequences.
telling a lie would turn his stomach sour.
he would hold doors open for women
and be allowed to cry.
he'd grow to love himself
but in a way where he knew how
to properly love others.
and later on in life,
he would know how to love his wife
and he really would
forsake all others.
he'd love his daughters well
and there would be no void to pass on.

when my time is done here,
don't spend money
on elaborate headstones
or fancy caskets.
let my body return to the earth.
let my ashes
mix with the roots of a tree
so brand new with life,
right at the spot
where my life force ends
and the tree's begins.
so one day
the tree will be grand and tall,
a safe place where my children
can sit in the shade
and tell their children
stories about me.
and their children after that.
that is all the immortality I need.

poem inspired by Ashley Hise

jessica jocelyn

verse 2

girl (remastered)

behind every late diagnosed woman
is a little girl
who knew this world
was never made for her
but could never explain why.

I was a difficult child.
and by difficult, I mean
I'd refuse to enter buildings
if the smells
became too much,
grab me by my vertebrae
and freeze me in place.

I was a strange child.
and by strange, I mean
I had so much to say
that all the words
crowded my throat
and nothing
ever got through.

I hold my spinning head
in my hands.
let it pass,
let it pass,
let it pass
say it three times,
make it come true.
intrusive thoughts
smack me in the face,
begging to be acknowledged.
grasping me by the throat,
wanting to be purged.
let it pass,
let it pass,
let it pass.
say it three times,
make it come true.

I'd watch how people talked to each other. how they stood, what they did with their hands. how much eye contact they'd make. when it was appropriate to start talking and when it was appropriate to listen.

I was masking long before I ever knew that's what I was doing. I mirrored other's interests and hobbies. theirs became mine. and I'd learn everything I could about it. and when they'd leave, I didn't know who I was without them. or if I had any hobbies or interests that only belonged to me.

I would come home and collapse, exhausted. and not sure why. I didn't realize how much work I had put into myself just to be able to live in this world that I knew would never be big enough for me.

girl (remastered)

I was told tomorrow
will always be brand new,
a fresh beginning.
how can I put hope in tomorrow
when it looks just like
yesterday
and the day
before that?

when I tell people I'm autistic,
there's a pause.
they look me all over and then stare at me deeply in my
eyes, almost trying to find the autism in me.

"you don't look autistic at all!" they exclaim as they half
expect me to start putting on a show, not realizing that I
already am, almost like they need some sort of proof.
maybe even something that matches what they've seen on
tv.

or they make some attempt to try
and understand
even though they have no idea
what it's like
to be so uncomfortable
in your own skin,
or feel so alone
when you're surrounded by people.

I force a smile
because it's socially appropriate,
but holding it in place
makes me physically hurt.
why am I making myself
feel pain
just to make others feel comfortable?
look them in the eye,
one, two, three,
look away.
I'm not even sure
where I learned how to do this.

if the whole world
is a stage
and everyone is just
playing their parts,
then I must've missed the meeting
where the scripts
were handed out.
because everyone seems to know
what to do,
and most are so good at it.
and I have no idea
what's going on.
where do I stand?
what do I say?
damn, I wonder when that meeting was.

they say it's a spectrum,
but my mind is all about extremes.
to feel my sadness,
you'd have to drown in
the darkest of caves
and never have hope for the light again.
but to feel my happiness,
the way my whole body
buzzes with euphoria,
it's a blessing and a curse.
when I'm upset,
it's the saddest I've ever been.
but when I'm happy,
not even the sun shines brighter
than me.

relationships have always
been so confusing
because people
can never just say
what they mean.
if you're going to call me at 5:00,
and you never do,
and the reason is you *just didn't,*
I don't understand that.
why wouldn't you just call at 5:00?
or if you knew you probably wouldn't,
why say it at all?
it's always so hard,
I have no problem being
the girl of your dreams
over the phone or through text,
but when I'm in front of you,
now everything's different.
now I'm processing looking at you
and talking at the same time.
and you'd think that wouldn't be a struggle
but it is.
virtual me and physical me
are just two different people
and sometimes you don't get to have
the version of me
that's both of those merged.

I was told to be myself,
but not too much.

I was told to speak up,
but not be too loud.

I was told to look people
in the eye,
but not so much
they think you're weird.

it's not that I want
so desperately to be most popular,
it's that I'm just trying to get by.
to able to function
in school, at work.
to be able to talk to the cashier at the store
even though I wish they'd stop talking
because I don't want to hold
a conversation
that has no specific end result.

girl (remastered)

I mourn
for the freely autistic person
I could've been.

somewhere out there,
in another time and place,
I find out I am autistic at the age of 7
instead of 35.
I have a therapist who helps
walk me through panic attacks
so I don't always think I'm dying.
my parents understand
that some smells make me physically ill
and understand why I don't like
the way certain foods feel in my mouth.
they don't embarrass me when strangers ask
why I won't talk to them.
I am given the support to help me
find friends who will love me and not use me.
I grow into who I am
instead of fighting against it,
not even sure what I'm battling against.
somewhere out there,
in another time and place,
I always know who I am
instead of trying to become
what society thinks I should be.

girl (remastered)

I was sitting on the bus after school with my friend and my favorite song came on the radio. I felt so excited I started to bounce on the seat. a boy across the aisle looked at me and said, "you're weird."

I stopped bouncing and looked over at my friend and asked her if she thought I was weird.

"yeah, I think you're sort of different. but everyone knows you're weird, it's not a big deal."

I looked at things differently from that point on. I joined sports even though I was painfully bad at them. so, I got into the arts where I was better. and I felt that if I excelled and the spotlight was on me, I could pass as normal. so, I would try out for every solo that I could. and in high school I would make sure my outfit and hair and make-up were perfect because maybe that made me look normal too. I would make charts to make sure I didn't wear my "safe" clothes too often because other girls were quick to notice and point that out.

when I realized I was autistic, I knew there would always be something that separated me from people who weren't.

no matter what I did, no matter how hard I masked, I would always be different.

because I am.

me unmasked

is more interesting anyway.

late diagnosis is both
a celebration
and mourning.
I feel I now have all the pieces to my life
I always knew were missing.
everything has clicked into place,
levels of me are now unlocked.
but who am I?
without the mask, who am I?
how beautiful I get to find out,
but how awful to know I was mistreated
just because I was misunderstood.
I may seem more autistic now
than I did as a child,
but that's because I'm no longer hiding.
I was never broken like I thought.
I was never too much.
I was just undiagnosed.

I saw her sitting there,
a younger, smaller version of me,
at 9 years old, sitting on my childhood bed.
I slowly walked to her and knelt.
I took her hands in mine.
she looked up at me
and with a small voice asked,
"does it get any better?"
I squeezed her hands.
"not for a long time. it doesn't get better
for a long time."
she closed her eyes and tears
streamed down her face.
I let go of her hands
and placed mine around her small face.
"does anyone end up saving us?" she softly asked.
I smiled.
"yes." I said.
she then looked at me, hopeful.
"who saves us?" she asked.
I smiled even bigger.
"we do. we save ourselves."

jessica jocelyn

bridge

jessica jocelyn

where did you learn that you are unworthy?

it might have all started as an infant, held by a strange man in a robe. washing my forehead with warm water, speaking of not deserving my creator's love.

or maybe it was as a small child, being yelled at to honor thy father and thy mother as a hand smacked across the back of my head.

or perhaps as a teenager, sitting before a panel of men, proving I was old enough to partake in emblems I would never be good enough for.

or could it have been as an adult, listening to elders tell me I would struggle because I could never make as much money as a man could.

from the very beginning, I was taught I didn't deserve the life that I never asked for.

my grandmother
was one of my favorite people
but she carried a lot with her.

I never wanted to add to that.

I didn't talk to many people
about things that happened to me
as a child.
but sometimes I'd tell her
and she'd hold me
and tell me to pray more.

I never told her
that I was proof
no one was listening.

I never wanted to break her heart.

dear god,

when this is all over
and everything fades to black,
it's going to hurt so badly
if it turns out
you are real.

when I think of how
other people have their faith
sometimes it feels like
I'm a flightless bird
surrounded by other birds
high above me
in the sky.

I'm envious of how
it is so natural to them,
a part of their DNA,
but not a part of mine.

I know I may look like them
but I just wasn't made
to do what they do
and no matter how hard I try
I'm never going to be
one with the sky
like they are.

girl (remastered)

mama said I came from hell
with dark hair
and dark eyes
dark enough to never see any light.

so years later
when I would pray
and nothing changed,
I figured god knew
where I had come from
and knew
he shouldn't listen.

when I say I can't accept a god
who forgot all about me,
the response I get is:
"not my god. my god would never."
then whose god was it?
whose god allowed me
to cry myself to sleep,
begging him to come save me as a child?
whose god listened to my prayers
and watched me sit and wait for answers?

"god took away my mother's cancer. praise be."
what about my mother-in-law?
she was the only friend I had
in the whole world.
why didn't he save her?

"that's not how it works."
well please explain it to me then.
please make it make sense
to my broken heart
because it's easier to accept
that I was praying to someone who wasn't real
than to be praying to someone
who just decided to help
someone else and not me.

girl (remastered)

I am drawn
to the broken,
the bent,
and the forgotten.
the ones who know
how to fight for their lives,
the ones who weren't sure
they could make it another day.
the ones that know
what it's like to live after loss.
they appreciate every ounce of color
because they know what it's like
when the world turns dark.
to be loved by them
is to be swallowed up with a passion
I could never feel
with someone
who's never known pain or grief

I might not have religion
the way you do,
but I do know I have my sister.
and if hell is real,
I'm pretty sure we've already
walked through it
hand in hand.
so it will do you no good
to threaten me
with a place we've already conquered.
I don't have to walk by faith.
I walk by her.

sometimes I feel so sure
none of this is poetry.
and it never could be.
I was simply a child.
one that died many different deaths,
but none of them
were final and merciful.
and after every death,
there was nothing but laughter,
some sick sense of humor
wondering how I could still be alive
but so dead inside.
and all this happened
while everyone
and everything watched-
trees,
the rain,
the air,
god,
people who should've stepped in.
am I angry?
of course.
but anger fuels my existence
however meaningless.
I am alive just to spite
all those who wished
I was dead.

I don't think
I'm very good
at this game
we call life.
every time someone hurts me,
I apologize.

I must work
so hard to be okay:
the inner work,
the therapy,
taking care of my body.
it's so much work
and at the end of the day,
I'm exhausted.
but it's all worth it.
the people that love me,
the ones who share
their life with me
don't deserve
the unhealed version of me.

girl (remastered)

I carry everyone's baggage
for them
like they just showed up
at my house
after a long flight.

they say drowning is silent.
I tried to scream,
but no sounds can ever escape
when you're underwater.

when someone gives me
their heart,
I don't know how not to
crawl inside,
learn all I can
and carve wounds so deep,
it leaves the most beautiful
and tragic of scars,
hieroglyphs,
ones that future lovers wonder about.

who was she?
they will ask.

and he will whisper:
everything and nothing.

I have one foot
stuck in sadness,
while the other foot
is in the doorway to happiness.
parts of me dance
in the sunshine,
while the other parts
drown in the rain.
I am the one in the room
who laughs the loudest
while the grief stings
and pulls me backward.
I exist simultaneously
happy and sad,
and at any given moment
either one can take over.
don't try to pull me
one way or the other,
because one can't
exist without the other.

girl (remastered)

when my world ended,
I set it on fire
and danced in the flames.
the girl I used to be
turned to ash
and blew away in the wind.

people stare at me
like my trauma
is the sickness,
and forgiveness
for my abuser
is the antidote.

but I am not sick
and there
is nothing in me
to fix.

out of all the roads I could take,
regret is one
I don't want to go down.
never did I want to look back and say:
damn, that could've been me.
I could've been someone.

I was told I needed to forgive
to heal
and that everyone deserves forgiveness.
it was pressure
and weight on my shoulders,
an added suffocating responsibility.
one day,
I said out loud the things that
happened to me.
it made them real.
with a deep breath,
I released myself
from the burden given to me,
this idea that
forgiveness is required
to move forward.

girl (remastered)

I've been treating my grief
and my healing journey
like a race to the finish line.
trying to short-circuit my mind
to already arrive
at the part where
I'm happy and smiling.
today I will remember
to stop and pause,
sit in the tears,
breathe in the hurt.
the part where I come out on top
and stronger will come one day.
just not today.
today is for honoring the place
I am at right now.

and no one needs to understand that but me.

I am easy to love
and sometimes not.
my laugh is exactly like my mother's,
the very sound my father ran from.
and my eyes are the same color
of the man she hates most.
I am the product of a previous marriage,
a fact my step-father
could never swallow.

I've saved my own life
so many times
when I put
pen to paper
instead of blade to skin,
to bleed on these pages
instead of deep in the earth.
because how many times
have these words
pushed others
towards another day?
I'd walk through these broken roads
in every lifetime
if it means
that I save others.

dear anger,

sometimes I think something is wrong with me when I wonder why I can't let go of what people have done to me. and then I realize, it's not what they've done that I can't let go of.

it's you.

you are the ghost from my past I still can't chase away. just when I think you aren't around anymore, there you are. haunting me. I know if I just let you go, I can be set free. but I can't. I feel that you protect me. you remind me what people are capable of. you help me keep them at a distance. I hope one day, you and I can have peace. until then, at least I realize why you are still hanging around.

dear 2020 me,

I know you are broken.
and I know the pain is so bad that you can't breathe.
but breathe anyway.
get off the floor.
put one foot in front of the other. you have
work to do and someone to fall in love with.
that person being you.
brush her hair and nourish her body.
because you are going to do everything
they said you couldn't.
and you need to prepare.
because you are going to fight like hell.
and I need you to fight.
and this pain? I'm sorry to tell you
it doesn't fully go away. you're going to carry it
for a long time. but you are going
to get good at it.
it fuels your soul to where there is nothing
but beauty surrounding you.
so much beauty.
so please keep going.
you deserve everything on the other side of this.
you deserve to make it through.

love,
me

jessica jocelyn

outro

jessica jocelyn

there's so much courage
in deciding
to love again
after your heart shatters.
there's so much strength
in choosing to put all those pieces
back together
when someone
has given you
every reason not to.

why do we constantly hide
the fact that we are alive?
spending so much money on creams
to smooth the wrinkles,
dye away the grays,
slice away callouses on our feet,
running from time
as if we could ever outrun it.
maybe we hide the signs of being alive
because we know we aren't actually living.
constantly in the grind of "life,"
or maybe just the idea of what
we think it should be.
a rat race to the finish line
when we aren't even sure
what that finish line looks like.
maybe one day we will reach that point
when we stop hiding the signs,
maybe then we will start to live.

girl (remastered)

sweet one,
your childhood was bad,
but don't let that determine the rest of your life.
you had no control over your childhood;
don't let them take the part of your life
when the control is all yours.

one day,
you will look back
on all this mess
and you will
find the silver lining.
the tiny gifts
you took with you,
the lessons
you had to learn.
because no one is born
knowing these things
and sometimes all you end up with
is a shadow of your heart.
I promise
one day you will find beauty
and you will laugh
and you will cry as you look around
and think

damn, I'm glad I'm still here.

to the one with such a big heart:

be careful when someone
shows you the pieces
of their broken heart
but hasn't decided
to try and heal it yet.
it's an invitation
to their storms of misery
that they would
like to dance
with you in.

life has a funny way of teaching us things.
no one falls in love and yearns
for them to break their heart.
we don't enter situations expecting the worst.

until one day we do.

and we find ourselves tiptoeing into rooms,
hiding our smile,
turning away from a kiss
expecting a serpent's tongue
to come with it.

I hope one day you stop.
I know it hurts;
I know it's not fair.
but one day I hope you enter rooms loudly again.
I know you didn't expect for your life
to turn out this way.
but I hope you find the beauty in it again.
there is still so much beauty left to find.

some days you are conquering mountains,
other days it hurts to breathe.
both days,
you are enough.

there is something
to be said
about not becoming
just like those
who traumatized you
and all the work
you put in
to make sure that never happens.
that shit is not easy.
be proud of yourself.

remember,
no matter
how old you get
you'll always be the child.
it will never be on you
to fix the broken relationship
with your parent.
that will always be on them.

when I was 14, I joined a new church. the other girls looked at me but decided I just wasn't going to be welcomed. only one of the girls came up to me and we became instant friends. more than 25 years later, we are still friends.

in high school, my best friend gave me a CD and said to listen to it. I did and to this day, it's still one of my favorite bands. when I want to tell someone that I love them, I send them songs to listen to.

when I was 22, I went to the ER a lot because I thought I was having heart issues and didn't understand I was having panic attacks. I was given a teddy bear so I wouldn't feel alone. my son now sleeps with it, and I am instantly taken back to how loved I felt when I was 22 and again in the moments that my son offers him to me.

some moments feel simple, and you may not think you will leave an impact on people. but sometimes the little things end up being the big things. people never forget how you made them feel, and like it or not, they will carry a piece of you always. make sure it's a positive one.

life gave you a raw deal
and a bad hand,
but stop trying to look
for who you used to be.
she's not there anymore,
and she's not coming back.
instead,
here you are now
still pushing through
even though you went through
so much.
things meant to destroy you
only left you bent.

you cannot win
with people
who choose
to always see the bad
in anything you say.

you cannot reason
with people
who choose to stay
in their misery
because it feels
most comfortable.

people's inability to love you
does not equate
to your failure.

the door to healing
is always open to you.
you just have to
walk through it.

I am nothing
if I don't share all this.
these stories,
these moments-
because long after my body
fades away,
my words will linger
and help,
and protect,
and heal.
and oh, my dear,
will they heal.

and then one day I found her.
I found god just sitting there,
almost like she was expecting me.
to my knees I fell, sobbing.
she knelt beside me
and put a hand on my shoulder.
"say it. say it all," she whispered.
choking through my tears,
I screamed.
as she took me into her arms,
I pounded my fists into her chest,
her hair circling us both in the wind.

"where were you?!
how dare you show yourself now!
now that my hair has become silver
and wrinkles line my face!
I don't need you now!
I needed you then!"

she took my face into her hands
and gently wiped my tears.

"sweet girl, why did you wait?
all this time, why did you wait to be saved?
the power is yours.
and look…
you did such a beautiful job."

I got up and broke free from her.
I started to walk away and she tried to follow.
I held up my hand.
"stop," I quietly said.
"it's me that's walking away this time."

alone in the car,
radio high to the sky,
song on repeat,
not loud enough to hide my screams.
screams that wake
the girl inside who was sleeping.
my foot isn't heavy enough
to break the sound barrier,
but my mind will take me past it, instead.
a woman screams like this once,
and only once in her lifetime.
when the sound ends
and her eyes open again,
she's not that girl anymore.
she is a girl (remastered)
unabridged
unchained
unhinged
not living for you anymore
but living for her.

girl (remastered)

other titles by the author:

the author's personal journey of the building, destruction, and reconstruction of a family affected by addiction told through poetry

jessica jocelyn

finding
daisies

decorations by
janelle parraz

poems about breaking the cycle
and healing your inner child

jessica jocelyn

encontrando
margaritas

decoraciones de janelle parraz

the Spanish version of Finding Daisies

girl (remastered)

ABOUT THE AUTHOR

Jessica Jocelyn is the author of 3 poetry books (Chasing Wildfires, Finding Daisies, and Girl (Remastered), a proud mother, and a nemophilist. By sharing her lived experiences, she strives to deeply connect with her readers and remind them that they are not in this alone. Jessica's poetry may be hard to hear at times, but it's always healing to read. In the same vein, her past may be dark, but writing serves as her spark of sunlight. When she isn't storytelling, you can find this free spirited goth spending quality time with her family that inspire her every day.

 @jessica.jocelyn

@letters.to.anna

Printed in Great Britain
by Amazon

29762141R00094